Severe Weather

Tornadoes

by Trudy Becker

I0877599

FOCUS READERS
SCOUT

www.focusreaders.com

Copyright © 2026 by Focus Readers®, Mendota Heights, MN 55120. All rights reserved. No part of this book may be reproduced or utilized in any form or by any means without written permission from the publisher. No part of this book may be used or reproduced in any manner for the purpose of training artificial intelligence technologies or systems.

Focus Readers is distributed by North Star Editions:
sales@northstareditions.com | 888-417-0195

Produced for Focus Readers by Red Line Editorial.

Photographs ©: iStockphoto, cover, 1, 7, 11, 12 (bottom), 15, 16 (bottom left), 16 (bottom right); Shutterstock Images, 4, 8, 12 (top), 16 (top left), 16 (top right)

Library of Congress Cataloging-in-Publication Data
Names: Becker, Trudy author
Title: Tornadoes / by Trudy Becker.
Description: Mendota Heights, MN: Focus Readers, [2026] | Series: Severe weather | Cover title. | Audience: Grades K-1
Identifiers: LCCN 2025022912 (print) | LCCN 2025022913 (ebook) | ISBN 9798889986300 hardcover | ISBN 9798889986379 paperback | ISBN 9798889986508 ebook pdf | ISBN 9798889986447 hosted ebook
Subjects: LCSH: Tornadoes--Juvenile literature
Classification: LCC QC955.2 .B43 2026 (print) | LCC QC955.2 (ebook) | DDC 551.55/3--dc23/eng/20250813
LC record available at https://lccn.loc.gov/2025022912
LC ebook record available at https://lccn.loc.gov/2025022913

Printed in the United States of America
Mankato, MN
012026

About the Author

Trudy Becker lives in Minneapolis, Minnesota.

Table of Contents

What Are Tornadoes?

The air is windy.

The sky is full of **clouds**.

A dark cloud reaches down.

It spins fast.

The spinning cloud moves.

It rushes over the land.

It is a tornado.

thunderstorm

How Tornadoes Form

A **thunderstorm** grows.

Big clouds form in the sky.

Warm air moves up.

Cold air moves down.

The air starts to spin.

It goes faster and faster.

It makes a **funnel**.

Then it touches the ground.

funnel

Keep Safe

Tornadoes are strong.

They can break houses.

They can rip up trees.

Stay inside.

Keep away from the **window**.

Wait until the storm passes.

window

Glossary

clouds

thunderstorm

funnel

window

Index